Rip and Kat are tailors!

They make things every day.

Now they are on their way

to their shop.

Find the missing house on page 3.
Then cut and paste it into the town below.

Example

Rip

Ike

Kat

Ace

1

R&K Tailors

Rip and Kat have a tailor shop. Their shop is in the middle of the town and has a yellow roof.

 Find the missing signs on page 3. Then cut and paste them onto the shops below.

Example

Use these items for pages 1 to 11.

Cut this line ▬▬▬ .

To parents: Cut this line ▬▬▬ for your child.

↓ **Page 1** House   **Pages 2, 5** ↓ Signs

↓ **Pages 6, 7** Sweaters

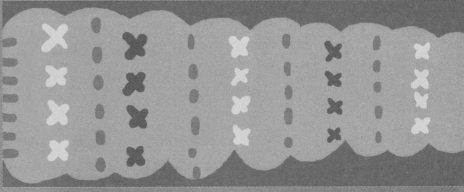

↑ **Pages 8, 9** Skirts

↑ **Pages 10, 11** Hats

Find the missing sweaters on page 3.
Then cut and paste them onto the snakes below.

Example

Next the Rabbit Sisters come into the shop.

"Hello! Do you have cute skirts for us?" ask the Rabbit Sisters.

Find the missing skirts on page 3. Then cut and paste them onto the rabbits below.

Example

Example

9

Now the Sheep Family needs some help.

"We want some wonderful hats," says the Sheep Family.

Find the missing hats on page 3.
Then cut and paste them onto the sheep below.

Example

Example

11

sheep below.

"Look at all the trees!" says Kat.

Find the missing trees on page 13.
Then cut and paste them below.

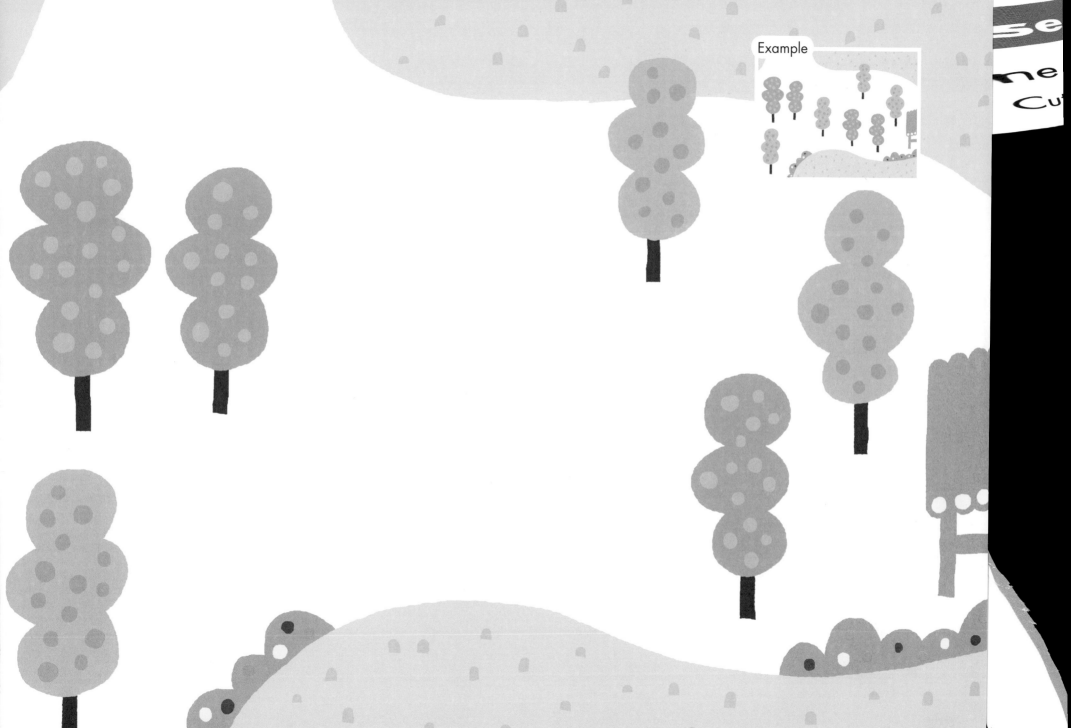

Example

Then cut and paste them below.

Example

For lunch they have muffins.

"Let's eat!" says Kat.

Find the missing muffins on page 21. Then cut and paste the muffins so that Rip and Kat are eating them.

Find the missing muffins on page 21.

Example

20

For dessert they have ice cream. "What is your favorite flavor?" asks Kat.

Find the missing ice cream on page 21. Then cut and paste the ice cream so that it sits on the cones.

Find the missing ice cream on page 21.

Example

24

"I'm full! Let's take a walk," says Rip.

"What nice flowers!" says Kat.

Find the missing flowers on page 21.
Then cut and paste them into the garden.

Find the missing flowers on page 21.

Example

26

Example

Now it's time to go back to work.

"Let's clean up the dishes!" says Rip.

Find the missing dishes on page 21.
Then cut and paste them into the basket.

Find the missing dishes on page 21.

Example

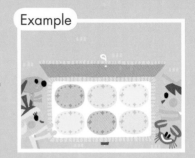

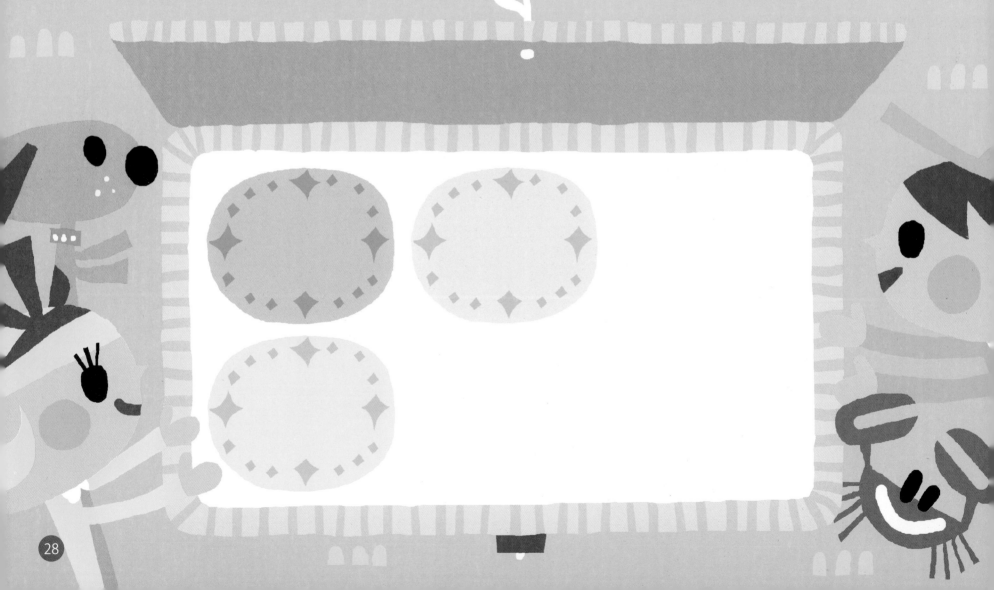

28

The King's Birthday

Today is the King's birthday!

The King asks Rip and Kat to come help at the castle.

Find the missing gate on page 31.

Then cut and paste it onto the wall.

Find the missing gate on page 31.

Example

Rip and Kat find the butler in the castle.

"We need hats for the guards!" says the butler.

Find the missing hats on page 31.
Then cut and paste them onto the guards.

Find the missing hats on page 31.

Example

Use these items for pages 29 to 37.

Cut this line ▬▬▬ .

To parents: Cut this line ▬▬▬ for your child.

↓ **Pages 30, 33** Hats

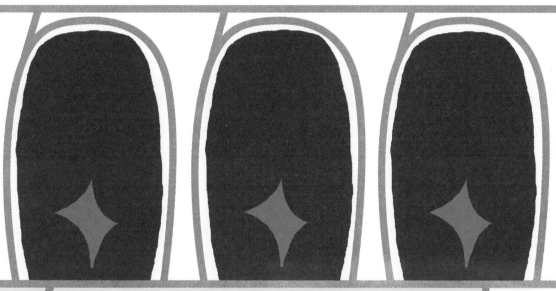

↓ **Page 29** Gate

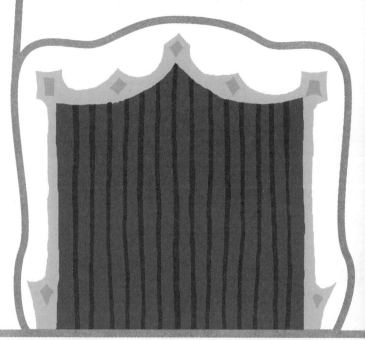

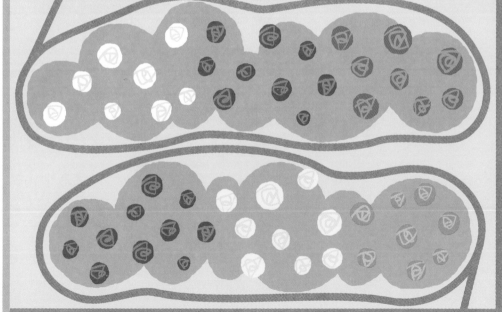

↑ **Pages 34, 35** Roses

↑ **Pages 36, 37** Flags

31

Example

33

"Look at the big garden!" says Rip.

"We need more rose bushes!" says the butler.

Find the missing roses on page 31.
Then cut and paste them into the garden.

Example

34

Example

"Let's put our best flags up for the King's birthday,"
says the butler.

Find the missing flags on page 31.
Then cut and paste them onto the flagpoles.

Find the missing flags on page 31.

Example

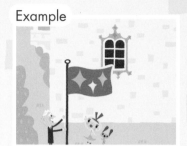

Example

37

Rip and Kat follow the butler into the castle.

Look at the princesses!

"We want new dresses!" say the princesses.

Find the missing dresses on page 39.
Then cut and paste them onto
the princesses.

Find the missing dresses on page 39.

Example

Now it's time to help the prince and the King!

"Please make us some cool pants," asks the King.

Find the missing pants on page 39.
Then cut and paste them onto the
King and the prince.

Example

Example

43

"Now we need cloaks to match our pants!"
says the King.

Find the missing cloaks on page 39.
Then cut and paste them onto the
King and the prince.

Example

44

Example

45

Then it's the Queen's turn.
"I would like the crown with
the most jewels, please,"
says the Queen.

Example

"We want crowns too, please!"
say the princesses.

Find the missing crowns on page 39.
Then cut and paste them onto the
Queen and the princesses.

Find the missing crowns on page 39.

Example

Now the guests are arriving for the party! Some clowns perform for everyone. "Make us some funny hats!" say the clowns.

Find the missing hats on page 49. Then cut and paste them onto the clowns.

Find the missing hats on page 49.

Example

Use these items for pages 48 to 56.

Cut this line ▬▬▬ .

↓**Pages 52, 53** Tails

↑**Pages 48, 51** Hats   ↓**Pages 54, 55** Candles and Cookies   ↓**Page 56** Presents

Example

51

Look at all the dancing animals!
There are monkeys and squirrels
and raccoons.

"Please find our tails!" say the animals.

Find the missing tails on page 49.
Then cut and paste them onto the
correct animals.

Find the missing tails on page 49.

Example

Example

The King's cake comes out. It is time to celebrate!

It looks like the cake needs some more candles.

There are some missing cookies too!

Find the missing candles and cookies on page 49.

Then cut and paste the candles on the cake and the cookies on the dish.

Find the missing candles and cookies on page 49.

Example

54

Wow, look at all the presents for the King!

✂ Find the missing presents on page 49.
Then cut and paste them onto the King's floor.

Find the missing presents on page 49.

Example

56

The Present from the Sky

The Sun is watching the King's birthday party.

He wants to celebrate, too!

He invites Rip and Kat up to help him decorate the sky.

✂ Find the Sun's face on page 59.
Then cut and paste it onto the Sun.

"Let's take a balloon into the sky!" says Kat.

Find the missing baskets with Rip & Kat and Ike & Ace on page 59. Then cut and paste them onto the balloons.

on page 59.

Example

"There are so many nice balloons in the sky!" says the Sun.

Find the missing balloons and baskets on page 59. Find the missing balloons and baskets on page 59.
Then cut and paste them into the sky.

62

"Look at the people in the parachutes!" says Kat.

"Their parachutes have nice colors," says Rip.

 Find the missing parachutes on page 59. Find the missing parachutes on page 59.
Then cut and paste them into the sky.

Example

64

Now it is nighttime.

"Hello, Moon!" says Kat.

"Look at the rockets!"

says Rip.

Find the missing rockets on page 67. Then cut and paste them into the night sky.

Find the missing rockets on page 67.

Example

Use these items for pages 66 to 73.

Cut this line ▬▬▬ .

To parents: Cut this line ▬▬▬ for your child.

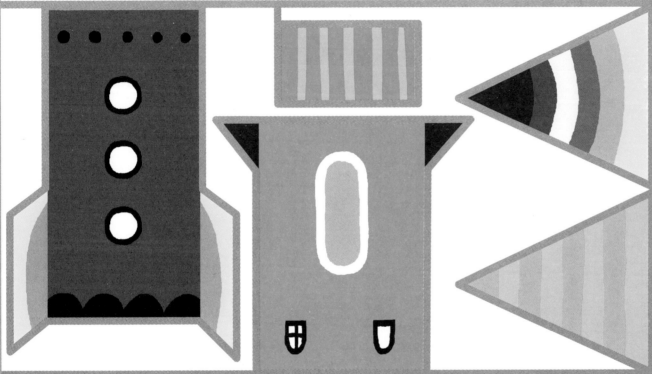

↑ **Pages 66, 69** Rockets

↓ **Pages 72, 73** Fireworks

↑ **Pages 70, 71** Bat and Owl

"Look at the bat over there!" says Rip.

"Who?" says the owl.

Find the missing bat and the owl on page 67.
Then cut and paste them onto their trees.

Find the missing bat and the owl on page 67.

Example

70

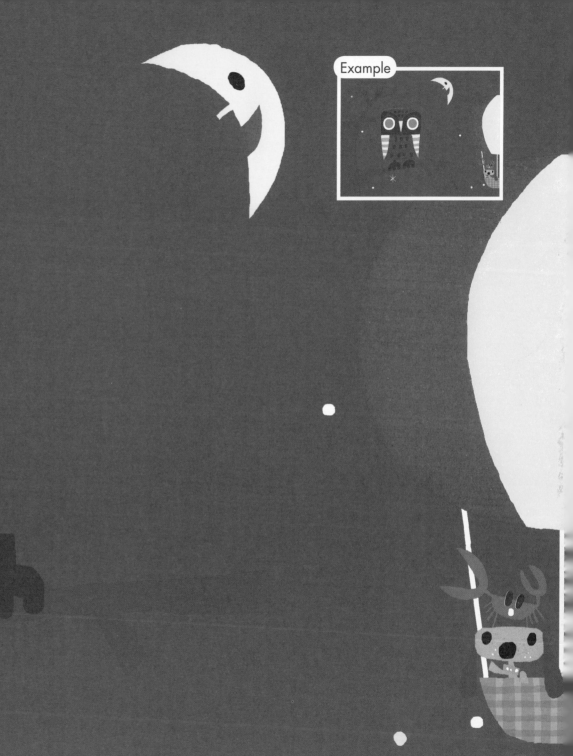

Example

71

At the end of the party,
the Moon sets off some fireworks.
"The fireworks are so colorful!"
says Kat.

Find the missing fireworks on page 67.
Then cut and paste them into the night sky.

Example

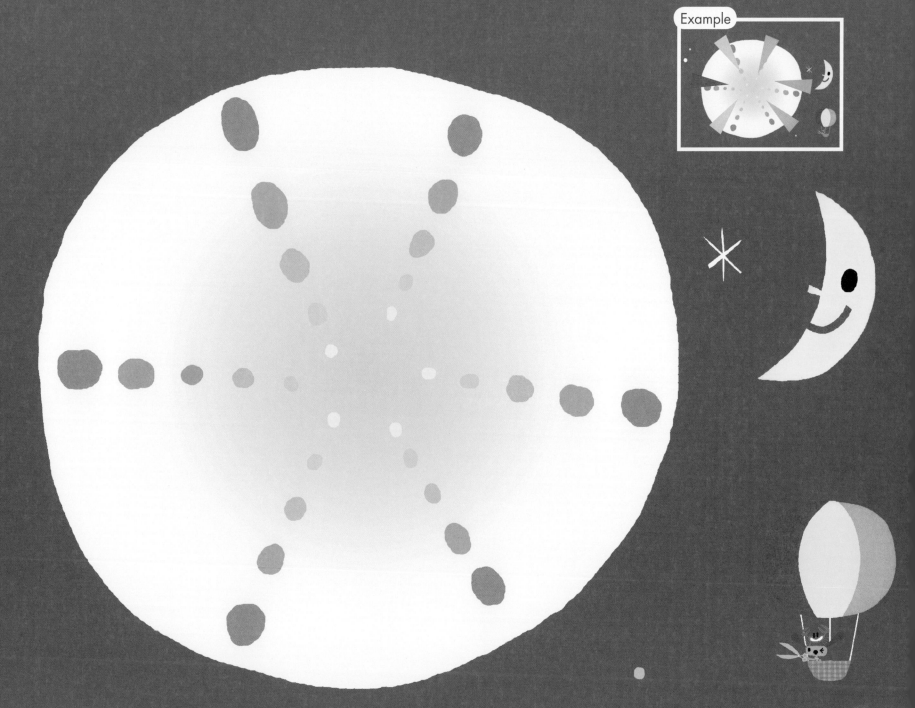

After a long day (and night!) of decorating for the King, the Sun and the Moon, Rip and Kat are ready to go home. "Let's go back to the shop," says Rip. First they have to fly over the road with all the cars.

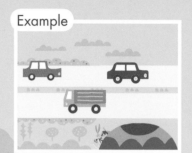

Example

✂ Find the missing cars on page 75. Then cut and paste them onto the roads.

Use these items for pages 74 to 80.

Cut this line ▬▬▬▬. To parents: Cut this line ▬▬▬ for your child.

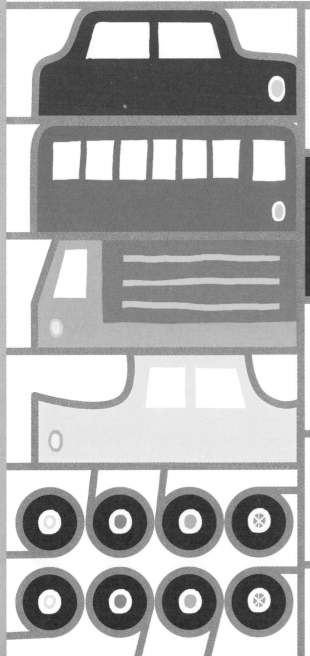

↑ **Pages 78, 79** Houses

↑ **Page 80**
Rip, Kat, Ike and Ace

← **Pages 74, 77** Cars

They land their balloon on the ground near town.

"Let's take the car back to the shop!" says Kat.

Find the missing houses on page 75.

Then cut and paste them into the town.

Example

Example

"What a great day of work!" says Rip.

"I wonder who will come to our shop tomorrow?" asks Kat.

Find Rip, Kat, Ike and Ace on page 75.
Then cut and paste them into the car.

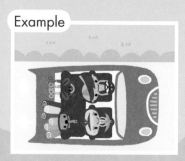

Example

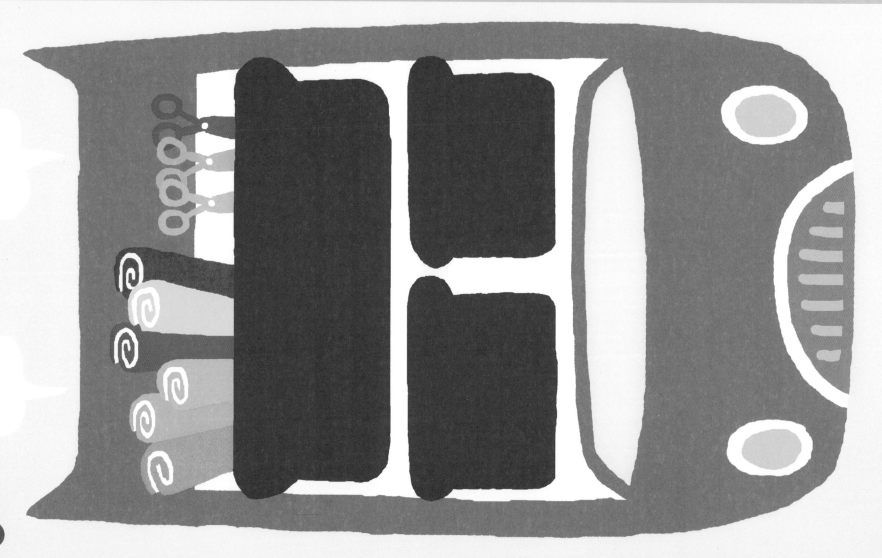

80